When a
SPOUSE
DIES

when a
SP🙢USE
DIES

WHAT I DIDN'T KNOW ABOUT
HELPING MYSELF AND OTHERS
THROUGH GRIEF

🙢 BARBARA R. WHEELER, DSW

PLAIN SIGHT PUBLISHING
AN IMPRINT OF CEDAR FORT, INC.
SPRINGVILLE, UTAH

ISBN 13: 978-1-4621-1666-9

Published by Plain Sight Publishing, an imprint of Cedar Fort, Inc.,
2373 W. 700 S., Springville, UT 84663
Distributed by Cedar Fort, Inc. www.cedarfort.com

The Library of Congress has cataloged the hardcover edition as follows:

Wheeler, Barbara Roberts, 1935- author.
  When a spouse dies / Barbara R. Wheeler, DSW.
     pages cm
  ISBN 978-1-59955-983-4
  1. Bereavement—Psychological aspects. 2. Spouses—Death—
Psychological
aspects. I. Title.
  BF575.G7.W46 2012
  155.9'3708655—dc23

                              2011043566

Cover design by Angela D. Olsen
Cover design © 2012, 2014 by Lyle Mortimer
Edited and typeset by Melissa J. Caldwell

Printed in the United States of America

10 9 8 7 6 5 4 3 2 1

Printed on acid-free paper

This book is dedicated to those who have lost and
grieved and who are
"like the bird that pausing in her flight awhile on
boughs too slight, feels them give way beneath her,
and yet sings, knowing that she hath wings."
— Victor Hugo

Going the far distance of knowing grief,
we find ourselves.

Praise for *When a Spouse Dies*

It is often difficult knowing how to respond to those who suffer heart-wrenching losses. This is a book about being sensitive and compassionate to others, as well as ourselves. This is not a "how to" book but rather one about the lessons grief and loss teach us. Dr. Wheeler's honest and open sharing of herself is a gift.

Richard Paul Evans, #1 *New York Times* bestselling author of *The Christmas Box* and The Walk series

When a Spouse Dies *is a gem of a book. Its pages are filled with wisdom and insight, for both the person feeling the death of a loved one and the person seeking to comfort the bereaved. Barbara Wheeler brings a special kind of knowledge to her subject. Not only is she a highly trained counselor in matters of spouse death, but she knows from wrenching personal experience what the loss of a beloved lifelong companion feels like. I found myself marking sentences on page after page, new truths that I wanted to print out and attach to my refrigerator door.*

Marilyn Arnold, award-winning author, *From the Heart*

There are few life events more widely experienced and yet more personal than the death of a spouse and the subsequent grieving of the partner left behind. . . . Dr. Barbara Wheeler's work is of significance due to her unique perspective and exquisitely reasonable approach. In this volume we hear the voice of a therapist combined with the real-life experiences of numerous widows and widowers, as well as tender observations of the author's own personal journey through loss. Readable, honest, warm, reassuring, and full of hope.

Virginia H. Pearce, bestselling author, *Glimpses in the Life and Heart of Marjorie Pay Hinckley*

CONTENTS

‮❧‬

CONTENTS

INTRODUCTION

Y *ou don't have to be a cow to know what milk is.* I often used this example in assuring my graduate students that they could help people with all kinds of problems, even though they may not have experienced them personally. They were preparing to become clinical social workers, and they needed the encouragement that they could do their jobs.

I always considered myself a competent, above-average teacher and therapist. But did I tell my students the truth? Could they lead clients through territory they had never known firsthand? Looking back, I question my instruction; I wonder about the effectiveness of my therapeutic interventions with people struggling with grief. While there is wisdom in the cow and milk illustration, the cow does have a significant "inside" perspective that we as consumers, or even farmers, cannot quite have.

The uncertainty about my past approach to directly helping clients, as well as students and friends, came when I was faced with the traumatic loss of my husband. I then realized that my "inside" perspective had been missing. I now have a deeper understanding of bereavement and see that I am better able to help others understand and cope with loss.

What would I do differently as a social worker, teacher, or friend when, metaphorically, I know what the cow knows? I would suggest to others that there are ways to compensate for incomplete life experience, but it demands a lot of them. They must learn to go to the depths of empathy, using their partial under-standing of loss to grasp a profound loss. I would tell them they must go to the far distances of knowledge about loss and the grieving process.

This applies on both sides of the equation—those bereaved and those extending guidance or comfort to the bereaved. And perhaps this applies to you, the reader, who has turned to this book possibly because the time is right.

Often our sorrows result from loss. As we journey

through life, we are bound to experience losses such as reduced income, family moving away, and failing health caused by illness, accident, or the natural aging process. If we live long enough, death will claim our parents and some friends. In some cases we may lose our children, siblings, and pets. Loss is not discriminating; it disrupts the lives of the young as well as the old. Loss can also come in the form of regrets—missed chances—memorialized in Robert Frost's "The Road Not Taken."

The extensive literature examining the grief process in humans and animals finds similarities with all kinds of loss. In humans, losing a child, parent, grandparent, sibling, friend, or pet can be equally painful. Some say that to lose a parent is to lose the past; to lose a child is to lose the future; to lose a spouse is to lose the present. While there is some truth in these observations, the loss of loved ones is much more complex. My hope is that readers suffering from grief of any kind will find helpful information throughout this book.

The loss of a spouse or partner is not easier or more difficult than other losses, but it seems to have a uniquely powerful and ruthless life-changing impact upon us. (Therein lies the passion for writing this book.) And I discovered in my discussions with those who have lost spouses that losing a wife may be subtly different from losing a husband. It also became clear that the experience of becoming widowed tends to vary with age and the stage in life—each with its own challenges.

Life's disturbing events are like photographs—moments preserved in time. We cannot change them, even if we wish to. When they are experienced, they may present mild challenges and temporary sadness or devastating chaos in our personal world. All and any reactions are normal and necessary to go through so that we can move on with our lives. Just like shaping and perhaps adjusting our response to the snapshots we revisit, the events of our lives take on the meanings we assign and reassign to them. Whether or not our remaining lives are fulfilling will depend on the significance we ultimately find in these crucial life episodes.

The synopsis is that loss and sorrow are impossible to escape in life. Grief is a common and normal reaction for all of us, yet each person will have his or her own manner of responding. We are all similar in different ways. Normalcy, with the recognition of differences among people, is a paradox:

each of us is unique yet we are all the same. Knowing that these two realities can—and do—coexist is essential as we navigate through our lives.

Within the chapters of this book, I have added to my own personal and professional experiences those of others who have lost spouses. The interviews I conducted with these men and women were not guided by scientific research, yet they yielded helpful, subjective information, giving a broader perspective to my understanding of loss and grief. Their stories are reported anonymously. It was interesting to find that the "I didn't know until it happened to me" factor was common among the widows and widowers alike. As one woman explained: "I feel so alone. It's like I'm the only person going through this—even if it's not true." One of the purposes of soliciting different points of view is to establish a degree of universality, giving some sense of normalcy and comfort to those feeling alone in their heartrending situations.

My optimistic expectation is not only that the grieving person will find help and comfort in these pages, but also that those who are helping others through the process will especially gain a sense of direction in their efforts to lend understanding and support.

Reading a book from cover to cover may be difficult for a person who is in the first stages of muddling through the loss of a loved one. Intense stress tends to affect concentration and retention. One woman reported that after her husband died, she sometimes would fall into an open-eyed trance reading lines of a poem or short story until her eyes lost focus—the letters separating from the words. If this is the case, I would suggest to read these pages in bits and pieces, gleaning what fits at the moment. At a later time, the book can certainly be reread in a different manner. It may end up serving as a useful reference for later times.

This is not a "how to" book. It is more of a "how it was done" collection of a few personal stories, with reflections on those accounts. In this way, readers can find solace in recognizing that they are not alone. From others' stories, they can pick and choose coping strategies for themselves while catching a glimpse of their own future possibilities. Most important, they will learn that along the way, they must accept and honor their *own* way of grieving.

I treasure lifelong learning. Curiosity, discovery, and understanding seem to nourish life in such a deliberate and restorative way—from beginning to end. I am grateful for the lessons learned from my own experience (wrenching as it was), as well as from others who have survived the loss of a spouse. These lessons appear throughout the book, particularly at the end of each chapter.

People are very uneasy talking about sadness. I learned from my work and experience that grief will never be a subject at social gatherings. People do not like to talk about loss, sorrow, or anything close to the subject. It is puzzling that a part of life so common, so normal, is "off-limits" for discussion. In that sense, this book challenges our comfort. I accept the challenge.

ONE

❧

I Didn't Know How Pervasive Grief Could Be

I don't know why I didn't know. When other afflictions invade the human body, spirit, and mind, their invasive attack is typically persistent. Cancer, depression, diabetes, poverty, heart and lung disease—any and all demand to be ever-present in our lives every minute of every day. Why not grief? Perhaps it is because we need to fully understand that grief has a life of its own. Like a drill sergeant, it insists on being in charge of our lives—for a *period of time.*

Before considering how grief plays out its "life," it is important to focus on some basics. Understanding ourselves and others who are grieving is the most important step in coping with bereavement. Grief can be placed on a continuum. Current psychological literature differentiates between grief that is "normal," "complicated," or "traumatic." Complicated grief includes the normal mourning process but it leads to chronic or ongoing mourning and often involves depression. Traumatic grief overlaps with post-traumatic stress disorder. It is in these cases that reactions to the trauma of the actual death are present. Both complicated and traumatic grief are rare and may require professional help. Normal grief, by definition, is not rare.

Grief is not depression. Although some of the symptoms are similar, depression is something quite different. Depression can involve chemical and physical change and is on-going, without periods of relief. Feelings of pervasive heaviness, worthlessness, and fatique don't always seem to have a point of origin or cause. It is sometimes accompanied by suicidal thoughts. All daily tasks seem insurmountable. With depression, the "will" is weak or gone, as is interest in life. Sadness is usually not the prevailing emotion, as one would assume. Rather, it is the inability to feel *anything* that is prominent. A sense of self—or ego— is seriously impaired; so is the intellect.

These characteristics are not common in grief where a deep, poignant sadness, most often focused on loss, prevails. Grief reactions (more than symptoms of depression) resemble those of shock and stress. Grief's pervasiveness includes a variety of feelings that seem to surge and recede, giving a false sense of relief before the next flood of emotion appears. A sense of self typically remains intact.

Grief, being self-directed, decides *how* it will manifest itself in each individual. The list of possible grief responses is never all-inclusive. Some people may not be affected by many of the "common" grief responses but find their pain carving dissimilar paths. Neither do their emotions occur in stages, as Elizabeth Kubler-Ross suggested several decades ago. We latched onto her theory, possibly because it helped us explain the pain, even though we wondered why our own grief wasn't following the formula. At the end of her life, Kubler-Ross did acknowledge that perhaps we all had relied too heavily on her explanation of the mourning process. In *On Grief and Grieving*, she maintained that the stages were "never meant to help tuck messy emotions into neat packages." The pervasive emotions inherent in grief are not only messy but also complicated and confusing, unlike other affective responses.

Grief is not a one-time thing but is a process that ebbs and flows. The emotions seem to attack in waves.

People whom I have talked with after losing a loved one consistently report the phenomenon of unannounced waves. They agree that there were times when they seemed to be in control of their thoughts, feelings, and behaviors as they went about daily activities. Then, without warning, a wave of emotion crashed over them, like flood waters without boundaries spilling over everything in their path. Suddenly they were out of control. We can be in charge of our thoughts and behaviors (even if it doesn't seem doable at times). But that we can be in charge of feelings like sadness and grief is an illusion. Grief is erratic. "You can't trust it," one woman observed. It often comes without a trigger, and if triggered, it's by very small things like a sock on the floor or the smell of aftershave.

I found that waves, resulting in crying spells—meltdowns—are, in fact, healthy in a therapeutic way. "Riding the wave," as any surfer will attest, is superior to—and safer than—fighting it. The good news about waves is that their intensity slowly diminishes over time, leaving a somewhat manageable undercurrent.

I didn't know about grief waves until I experienced them myself. The unexpected tears would appear, of course, at the least convenient times. One such moment was when I ventured to the bank after my husband's death. It was time to change our account into my name. The day wasn't particularly sunny—in fact it was a dusty elephant shade of gray. I should have taken the clue. (In my defense, I wasn't up to taking any clues.) I shuffled in the door, primed to conduct business as I had done so many times in the past. As the teller asked if she could help me, I felt my lip quiver and tears distort my vision. The colors on the marble-like counter began to run together. Did the teller's question set me off? Such a simple, unemotional greeting? I'm not sure if I was more caught off guard, embarrassed, or confused by the emotional attack. Grief was in charge. I was not.

Confusion during times of bereavement can be a symptom of stress. The stress of losing a spouse is enormous. Studying life-stress, Holmes and Rahe found that "death of a spouse" ranked as the most stressful of life experiences. "Death of a close family member" was fifth out of twenty-one identified variables.[1] Is it any wonder that typical stress responses such as anxiety, confusion, and loss of control are often the same as our responses to the death of a loved one?

It's a well-known fact that grief's major predecessor is loss. Devastating loss feels like a robbery. It steals a valued and irreplaceable part of our lives. The loss of a spouse leaves an anxious emptiness that is, at times, frightening. Fear and anxiety are so related that they feel one and the same. Some widows and widowers report anxiety attacks following the loss of their spouse. One woman described how astounded she was by the "enormity" of the loss itself. She "could never have predicted the intensity of the loss and length of time it took to come to grips with it." The time and intensity, of course, vary from person to person.

The fear that can coexist with stress and loss is similar to the apprehension felt in grief. When C.S. Lewis wrote of his wife's death in *A Grief Observed*, he began by saying, "No one ever told me that grief felt so like fear. I am not afraid, but the sensation is like being afraid."[2]

Lewis also told of a feeling similar to being mildly drunk with a sort of invisible blanket between the world and him—finding it hard to take in what anyone said. Similarly, it is common for others to report a "brain fog," describing an inability to think well or to focus their attention for any length of time. Even reading is laborious. One woman reported feeling "like something was broken inside my head." Another added: "It's like I had a mental illness." Some people don't realize they are in a brain fog at the time—until they are out of it, looking back. Perhaps it is because of this normal but strange haze eclipsing our thinking that grievers are counseled to postpone as many decisions as possible for the time being.

One of the grief "stages" identified by Kubler-Ross and others is anger. Some people do experience anger when losing a spouse, but it doesn't seem to be as common as was thought. Perhaps one reason is we have learned to see anger as a secondary emotion. This means other emotions are typically "under" (or precede) anger, such as loss, frustration, sadness, abandonment. These primary emotions need to be acknowledged and addressed in order to manage anger. A former client talked of her anger at God for taking her young husband. At the outset, with fists clenched and lips tight, she said: "It just isn't fair." When she came to realize the intensity of her feelings of *abandonment* and *fear* of being alone, her anger slowly dissipated. It was at that point that she began experiencing healthy grieving. Recognizing the intricacies of anger and related feelings can be helpful in healing from grief.

An older man, who lost his wife of fifty-four years was bothered by how pervasive his feelings of self-centeredness were. He asked: "Am I selfish— self-centered because I can't seem to stop thinking of the loss of my wife and how much I miss her?" Joan Didion wrote in *The Year of Magical Thinking*, "People in grief think a great deal about self-pity. We worry it, dread it, scourge our thinking for signs of it. We fear that our actions will reveal the condition tellingly described as 'dwelling on it.'"[3] Most of us grow up learning how adversative these personality traits are and that we should learn to avoid them and focus on concern for others.

There are times when conventional learning just doesn't fit. I assured this recent widower that when we are in such a crisis state, we *naturally* and automatically go into survival mode. This means our mind, body, and spirit shift into self-preservation. It becomes very difficult to think of and feel for others—not impossible, but extremely difficult. In a healthy recovery—however long that takes—we will return to increased caring for and about others. I reminded this particular widower that in a marriage or a long-term, intimate relationship, we are used to considering our partner in our daily decisions—directly or indirectly—often without being aware of it at the time. The impact of "I'm now totally alone; it's all up to me" takes some getting used to. So out of necessity, we focus on ourselves. Our own human nature is teaching us how to use this "new" autonomy, forced upon us, to survive.

A postscript to the above vignette is my observation that the men I interviewed most often used cognitive words such as "thinking," "thoughts," and "mind" to describe their inner grief experience. Women, on the other hand, used more feeling words like "pain," "overwhelmed," and "hurt." Additional male/female differences are discussed in chapter three.

So what did I learn about the "pervasiveness of grief" since adding "fellow traveler" to my professional title? I learned that grief is not a word—it's a force. In addition, I now grasp, even with conviction, the truth that grief and death are normal parts of life. I know that grief is *not* an enemy to us—even if it feels like a declaration of war. It is nature's way, *through a gradual process*, of helping us accept a devastating loss. Perhaps the more pervasive it is in the beginning, the sooner we can heal.

NOTES

1. Thomas Holmes and Richard Rahe, "The Social Readjustment Rating Scale," *Journal of Psychosomatic Research* 11 (1967): 213–18.

2. C. S. Lewis, *A Grief Observed* (San Francisco: HarperCollins, 1961), 3.

3. Joan Didion, *The Year of Magical Thinking* (New York: Alfred A. Knopf, 2005), 192.

TWO

❧

I Didn't Know the Intricacies of My Marriage

We've heard marriage referred to as a dance. We glide through life, leading and following in some kind of pattern we choreograph to fit our relationships. Like any dance, after we perform it for any length of time, our steps become automatic, thoughtless, and balanced.

For me, the success of the dance did not seem to depend upon a need to examine the intricacies of our steps. I became complacent at best, indifferent, at worst. I was too into it to be objective, anyway. Then my partner left the floor. The music stopped. The dance was over. How did that happen? What was it all about? Maybe I should have seen it coming earlier—been more aware. I never gave it a conscious thought that his steps forward resulted in—even required—my steps backward, then, by reflex, changing places. We needed to do that to give the dance balance. We *had* to take different positions, at any one time, and we did.

In marriage, it's our similarities that *bring* us together, our differences that *keep* us together. Differences add spice, interest, and life to the relationship. Yet I'm aware that too many intolerable differences will crumble the relationship. It's not that kind of variance that we're talking about here. The key is how we *handle* the differences, not that we do or don't have them. For most couples, the navigation around and through the differences creates the needed balance to their interactions. It seems when we are in a time-tested relationship, our differences will emerge as one partner counters the other's opinions with his or her own. When our partner leaves the "floor," everything seems to change. The balance is gone. No need for counterbalance anymore.

Several people I interviewed mentioned some sort of marital balance or counterbalance as memories carried them back through the years. The phenomenon was expressed in different ways, such as in a conversation I had with a recently widowed father of four. Planting flowers was an issue in his relationship. Every spring he would question why his wife would spend so much time, effort, and money on planting annual flowers, knowing they would last only until the first fall frost. When the next spring came, it started all over again. He thought the whole process was absurd. When I made my way on the stone path to his front door, I noticed an assortment of bedding plants all tucked tightly in their individual pots waiting to be rescued by an eager gardener who would plant them where they could stretch and grow. I commented on their splendor. His response? "Oh, well, what can I say? I don't know why I bought them or why I'll be planting starting tomorrow, but I will." Restoration of balance in the making.

I had more attempts to recreate equilibrium after my husband Jim died than I would like to acknowledge. Perhaps the most blatant one concerned our shower and his need to squeegee the glass doors after every use. I thought it was a waste of time and opted not to conform. The glass would only have wet spots come the next shower. "That's the shower door's job— to be wet," I would profess. So we agreed to disagree. He would squeegee after his shower, and I would not after mine. Silly stuff, right? It was only a few weeks after the funeral that I found myself using the squeegee following my shower. What was I doing? My behavior was 99 percent outside of my awareness. It was as though I woke up discovering myself behaving in this strange, detached way. I smiled. It was really quite humorous. Oddly, grief can have in it humor as well as grace. I guess it's because humor and death are both inescapable parts of life.

Was I, on some cognitive or emotional level, attempting to reconnect with Jim? I did feel closer to him by completing his valued shower task. I was representing his "side" of the argument. Why was I compelled to do that? Somehow, it didn't seem a waste of time at all. There is a need for all living things to gravitate toward homeostasis and perhaps his viewpoint needed to be represented and he was not there to do it. Balance was somewhat reestablished when the shower glass was clear.

As time went on, I discovered that I really didn't mind a clear glass shower door. In fact, it sort of made sense. I made that decision independently, sans a need for counterbalance. I took one small step forward in conducting my altered life. I no longer needed to make statements to establish my individuality in the context of my relationship. I took my stand based on more objective data. Was I starting to grow through loss?

Do I feel guilt about the disagreements I had with Jim? No. I know such sparring is as natural and normal as the dance itself. Not all of those left behind in a death feel this way. Guilt is mentally painful and powerful. It can "move mountains." This is not about the *constructive* guilt that keeps us from robbing banks. The guilt that sometimes haunts surviving spouses is *destructive* guilt. It can destroy relationships and people and override cherished memories.

More than once I heard former caretakers who had nursed a loved one over an extended period express some relief at the death of their spouses. The relief was entangled with profound sadness for their loss. The guilt they felt was for their own sense of freedom since the load had been lifted from them. Why wouldn't relief be an expected, normal response? It's no news that caretaking is one of the most difficult jobs on the planet. Most caretakers who were interviewed said they willingly, without a second thought, stepped up to the task. "I did it for *him*—not out of duty," one woman explained. "Love and commitment go a long way," she added. "But I'm exhausted—physically and emotionally." Another former caretaker agreed that "it wasn't a burden, it was a privilege, but

I felt the weight." She continued in a self-condemning tone, "I'm sorry to say that." Appropriate guilt? No. Isn't it normal to feel "exhausted," "burdened," and "weighted" down? Further kudos to these caretakers for having the courage and honesty to express their conflicted emotional anguish!

Guilt can also be attached to memories of things said or unsaid—behaviors we're not proud of. A couple had a disagreement about driving directions just days before the husband's expected death. The wife was able to tell him she was sorry, and he did the same. This led to a conversation about past disagreements, and each was given the opportunity to ask for forgiveness for those times. She said, for her, the sincere, emotional exchange was instrumental in avoiding guilt after he was gone.

And then there's *survivor's guilt*—"Why not me?" I experienced this personally, when I had such a strong desire to go with Jim. My place (and my perceived happiness) was with him. I have heard others express the same feeling. For me, however, it wasn't survivor's *guilt* as much as survivor's *yearning*—an indescribable empty, painful yearning. We had been together fifty-one years and my *place* was with him. We were a team. I couldn't imagine living without him. I didn't even want to try. Those were initial raw, knee-jerk thoughts and feelings that didn't last—thankfully.

The bottom line is that grief-related guilt is destructive. It can morph into self-punishment as quickly as anger turns to violence. It's also an exercise in futility—what's done is done. We just can't go there. All marriages have built-in minor (and some major) regrets because they're no more perfect than we are. Guilt, however, does have one redeeming feature—it teaches powerful lessons we can use as we move on through our lives. That is guilt's power. This mostly applies to guilt from things said or unsaid and behaviors we wish we could do over. The learning process goes something like this: First, we identify what is disturbing us. Second, we allow it to be in the past where it belongs. Third, we give ourselves credit for doing the best we can *at any given moment in time*. For example, no one ever says, "I think I will now make a mistake." It is unfair and unrealistic *to judge past behavior with present information*. One widow was punishing herself with guilt because she relentlessly insisted that her dying husband wear a mask of oxygen even though he didn't want it. He died soon after. "If I had only known he was that close to death," she lamented, "I wouldn't have forced the oxygen on him. I would have helped him to feel peaceful and calm. I feel terrible." She was judging—unjustly—her past behavior with information she acquired after (in the present).

The fourth and last step from guilt's lesson book is the extraordinary opportunity we have to transfer the corrected behavior to present or future interactions with others. A recent widower's story was a profound illustration of this. He told of his wife's ability to "smother others with kindness—especially in tense situations." He, on the other hand, would handle such situations with confrontation, saying things he later regretted. His anger had a short fuse and it often left him embarrassed and guilt-ridden. When he talked about how he had changed, he proudly reported, "I now do it her way. I like it. It feels better." Not only had he rectified his regrets and guilt over his past behavior but he had also learned from his deceased wife a new, more productive approach in his current and future interactions. (Could this also be an attempt to return to some sort of marital balance previously known to him?)

The emotions accompanying grief are so overpowering that practical concrete tasks following a death seem to find a place way beyond the back burner—especially at first. Or perhaps the "business" details are pushed out of sight and mind because of the wrenching pain stirred up by them. The eventual sorting of belongings—piece by piece—can be overwhelming. Joan Didion described the unrealistic thoughts following the death of her husband. She admitted, "I could not give away his shoes. He would need [them] if he was to return."[1] She knew the thought was irrational—but it was so real. After I had sorted through Jim's clothes and belongings (a wretched job), giving them to family members and friends, I noticed his shoes still in neat boxes on the closet shelf. Could this be why I had not given them away? If so, it would have been on some other level than a conscious one. So armed with some newly acquired insight, thanks to Didion, I packed up all of the boxes, including his most recently purchased shoes, a pair that had been worn only once or twice. When he brought them home, filled with pure joy, he'd said, "Aren't these the coolest shoes ever!" He was so proud of his purchase.

When I arrived at the Goodwill store, it was a cold, blistery winter day. The attendant picked the boxes from my car and tossed them into his big bin. I glanced over my shoulder just in time to see Jim's "cool" shoes take flight out of the box. I lost it. Emotionally, that was one of the most painful moments in my entire traumatic journey.

I learned it was okay to take my time sorting belongings. What was too painful today to sort would be there tomorrow. I needed to go at my own emotional pace. There was no requirement of when the job needed to be completed. Given that truth, I learned of one task that would not wait—paper work. You can find a plethora of advice from lawyers and financial consultants concerning necessary paper work surrounding the death of a spouse.

They usually urge us to get as much as we can in order before the death. Many of us don't do it. Some financial matters cannot be completed until after, such as social security arrangements. Without an exception, those I interviewed found the task to be daunting, exhausting, and, at times, endless.

Loss has taught me that the death of a spouse or partner affects every aspect of the day. The empty house sets the stage for constant, unwelcome reminders. However, the intricacies of a marriage seem to come into focus particularly at night, when loneliness and aloneness are all too clear. Others offer support, but at the end of the day, we go to bed alone—fending off self-pity and the cold.

I have tenaciously tried *not* to remember the dates of my parents' deaths. I wanted to remember their birthdates and their lives—not relive their deaths. But my husband's death date is beyond my ability to "forget." It haunts me when it approaches, as do other significant dates.

When one woman's husband died in a tragic accident after only ten years of marriage, she braced herself for the holidays ahead. "But it was the special dates—with our own private meaning—that caught me off guard," she explained. She wasn't prepared for grief's ambush on Father's Day, their wedding anniversary, their son's little league home run, or birthdays. These "celebrate us" family days were all supposed to be shared as married partners. It had been years since the accident, yet her eyes moistened as this suddenly single mother described how heartbroken she was for her young children on Father's Day. To get through the day, she planned a special family activity to be repeated for the next two or three years. For her own birthday, she learned that buying something for herself helped her to cope with the emptiness escorted by grief. Giving yourself a gift *does not feed self-pity—it prevents it.*

Under ordinary circumstances, holidays magnify everything. For those struggling with loss, the intensity can be overwhelming as we search for ways to get through it all. I am not quite ready to acknowledge that Valentine's Day is anything more than just another day. I cope by ignoring it. *Denial is not unhealthy as long as I am consciously aware of the choice I've made.*

A widower had just one Christmas wish: "Please let it be over." It seems like everything hurts at Christmas. Some attempts to ease the pain were offered by those I talked with:

- I found that I needed to be patient with myself—allow extra time to accomplish things.
- I discussed this with my family so they would know what to expect.
- I simplified things. I didn't send out Christmas cards or fix my usual big dinner.

- Attending a support group helped me. I also set aside grief time, and by doing that I felt more "in control" later on. (There might be a problem here in that grief may not cooperate—choosing its own time to erupt.)

- I tried to get extra rest because it seemed the stress was depleting me.

The question frequently arises: Is it better to keep holiday traditions as normal as possible or to do things differently (because they are different)? Most survivors agreed that if changes are made, it might be best to wait at least a year. Probably over time, some traditions will remain and others will change. Of course, all of us, I hope, will do what seems to fit for ourselves and our families. Certainly the ages of children will be a factor. The first family Christmas after Jim died, I bought plain white ornaments—one for each family member. I asked them to write a special memory of their dad or grandpa on their ornament and hang it on the tree. We then continued with our other time-tested traditions that Christmas as well as the following years. We have pensively made a few minor changes—moving us forward. The white ornaments remain on the tree every year.

The anticipation of the holidays ahead can be worse than the actual event. I remember the feelings of relief and bewilderment when I survived the dreaded days of "celebration." I now know (after the passing of time) that *significant dates need not be forgotten nor feared.*

Memories of past holidays are typically about closeness and are overpowering at first. A surviving spouse insisted that for others to "tell me that memories will sustain me is not helpful. I want *him*—not his memory." Her loss had occurred only a month before Christmas. For me, memories were too painful at first to be any comfort, especially on holidays. They gradually became tolerable, then treasured. Now I recognize they're definitely a significant part of my healing. It's as if, from the beginning, memories struggled to find a place in my grief. I fought them off. Now, every day, I welcome and cherish their sustaining power. It is also comforting for me to recognize that memories are a part of me and all I have become. In that sense, Jim is with me every minute of every day.

Loss and grief often result in retrospection of what was—that which was previously taken for granted. Lisa Marie Presley, former wife of Michael Jackson, admitted it wasn't the divorce that prompted her to examine the intricacies of her former marriage, but the death of Michael. It was then that she gained clarity about her relationship with him. A death tends to mysteriously open one's eyes, intellect, and heart like no other experience.

I have long professed my self-contained identity, happiness, and fulfillment. Because of my deep love for Jim, I cared about his happiness as much as, or more than, mine. *Caring about his joy did not diminish mine.* When he died, I realized how much of my life's activities and meaning were connected to him. With a bare minimum of self-awareness and fifteen years into the marriage, I would have readily denied this. So much of my daily nest-building energy—keeping an ordered, decorated, and clean house and preparing meals—was, on some level, for him.

Without Jim, my reference point was gone, as well as my best friend and the love of my life. I didn't seem to care if I ever replaced the old, shaggy sofa pillows or threadbare rug. I had to redefine the meaning of my life on many levels. What would I care about now that could fill the emptiness with some kind of significance? I'm in process on that one.

The intricacies of my marriage can be summed up with this realization: losing a spouse really is different from losing grandparents, parents, friends, pets, and siblings. I have had all of those experiences and all are extremely painful. But the loss of a spouse in death—the interruption of balance—introduces a long list of dynamics, unlike any other. At the top of the list, as my friend so poignantly framed it, is that "I miss being adored."

And I might add, I also miss *giving* that adoration. Reciprocal, marital love and devotion are powerful—defying substitution.

Finally, in reflecting on the intricacies of my own marriage, I learned that the death of a companion in such a loving relationship has some similarities with and differences from losing a spouse in divorce. The most profound difference is that while the divorcee at one time may have felt adored, love is close to the antithesis of divorce. Most often damage to self-esteem intensifies as the breakup unfolds. Divorce is not without grief—it's the death of a marriage, its hopes and dreams, that is the source of grief and pain for the disillusioned partners. In both divorce and the death of a spouse, love is wounded. *Grief is the price we pay for love*, as England's Queen Elizabeth so poignantly put it. In the death of a spouse, love is not lost as it is in divorce. It lives on in the heart of the survivor. Having your partner die in an atmosphere of mutual respect and deep, committed love, as tormenting as it is, should not be overlooked nor undervalued.

NOTE

1. Didion, *The Year of Magical Thinking*, 37.

THREE

❧

I Didn't Know How to Cope with My Own Grief and Loss

I should have known about coping, and I did—textbook style. But there was more to learn, and that's a good thing. However, having to learn by living it is not particularly a good thing.

Just as there are many different ways people react emotionally when mourning, there are also many and varied ways to cope with loss and grief. As days and weeks pass, people will stock their own "cope chest" with strategies that work for them. It is essential that each of us accept our own way of coping as the *best* way for us. There is no *one* correct or best way. One size does not fit all.

I have found in my personal and professional experience that people who accept the responsibility to fill their own cope chests still find solace in talking with others who know sorrow firsthand. It helps to not feel so alone, and as one woman said, "not crazy." There is a therapeutic advantage in sharing coping methods. In addition to not feeling so alone, there are other benefits, such as the release of thoughts and feelings while discovering what others found helpful in their journeys through sorrow. What was helpful for them *might* be useful for your own healing.

After talking with a number of people and comparing their experiences with mine, I've discovered similarities in answers to "What do I do *now*?" We all draw on any strength we have in reaching for self-preserving "lifelines." These resources help us survive from day to day—hour to hour. Some just appear to us, without our reaching. When that happens, survival becomes overwhelmingly poignant. Lifelines take different forms. The interviewees reported most often these four categories: talking (catharsis), religious faith, family, and friends.

Most people experiencing bereavement need to express their thoughts and feelings, but *not all* people. A few find other ways to cope with their grief. It isn't always that these survivors don't have a need to express their feelings of grief but rather that they may lack the experience or skill to do so. Their eyes tell of deep pain yet send a message, "I'd like to tell you, but I don't know how." So the widower, eyes fixated on his shoes, takes extraordinarily long walks— silently communicating with his pain.

The need for catharsis is not always a conscious one. Rather, it is more of a subconscious longing to release complicated, messy thoughts and feelings in an attempt to make sense of them. So much of what we feel, think, and do is outside of our awareness. Talking, although therapeutic, most often can be difficult. One woman who expressed it well candidly observed, "Even though it's painful, it's helpful pain"—her voice, diluted by grief, sustained by hope.

Expressing one's self is typically an integral part of moving forward toward healing. Within a few days after my mother suffered a stroke, leaving her without the ability to speak, my father suddenly died. Allowing sufficient time for her healing, my sister and I, leaning on each other for courage, went to the hospital to explain to my mother why her husband of over fifty years was no longer visiting her. It was the most heart-wrenching experience I had ever faced. Was I up to it? Our words were measured in order to keep our emotions in check. Upon hearing

the news, she began to cry, but because she was apha-
sic, she couldn't express her grief in words. So many
questions unasked—so many feelings and thoughts
unspoken. The tears told the story of her internal torment. It was at this point that my emotions refused to
be ignored. I went with them. Bowing my own head,
I said a silent prayer, asking for comfort and peace
for my mother. My eyes slowly opened in time to see
her take a deep, staccato breath, then close her eyes
in sleep.

It would be later, after my mother awoke, that we
attempted to be her voice, guessing what she might
like to say. We were accustomed to doing this since
her stroke. She could then, with a nod of her head,
verify whether we were correct or not. All three of
us knew the importance of talking through grief and
loss—in any way possible.

A concerned client once asked if it was okay to
talk with his deceased partner. It was comforting to
him in his mourning process. He told me, not without
diffidence, that he would often talk to photographs
of the deceased. His gaze drifted away from me and
focused on the trees outside his studio window as
he explained that he had never told anyone about
this before. I assured him that it was okay and even

a normal way to cope with the pain of loss. His shoulders dropped in relief. I added that if he really believed his partner was always actually in the room, it could be a problem. (Some might disagree.) He was quick to assure me that often it felt like his partner was there but he was aware that it was a photograph in his hand. The recognition of what is real and what is not is a key factor.

There is another red flag, not especially common, concerning talking through grief. It's called "ruminating." Of course the danger of excess exists in *anything* we do. Overtalking or fixating on the loss, especially as it goes on over an extended time, can be *counterproductive* to healing.

How long is too long? What is overtalking or ruminating? When does it turn into a "fixation"? Definitions of mental health do not include guidelines for the duration of grief. Ruminating is simply repeating over and over the pain and loss at the exclusion of other conversational topics. In this rare situation, a person becomes so focused or fixed on his or her inner and outer situation that the dynamic flow of life goes unacknowledged. In a word: the person is *stuck*. Needless to say, it is an unhealthy coping mechanism.

"How do I know if mine is a healthy or unhealthy

reaction?" a young, widowed client once asked. "And how can I keep from becoming 'stuck' in grief—not moving on?" With my therapist hat on, I explained, starting with the basics.

It's a control issue. Stress causes a sense of powerlessness, so our minds go into a heavy-duty control mode. The definition of control includes to "hold onto," so our minds cling tightly to the loss because to let go would feel like herding wild rabbits—powerless chaos. This happens when we lose a self-identity (like "victim") and have nothing to take its place. So we get stuck in that state, our words are repetitious, and we become fiercely focused on only one facet of our lives. The problem? Our minds have tricked us into thinking that by holding on, we are in control. But we are holding on to something we *cannot* control—the loss of a loved one. (On some level we know that, but it's hard to convince our minds.)

What to do now? I told my client that she could look to the well-known serenity prayer that is the most succinct and profound mental health "formula" available to all of us. It states, in part, that you need to *accept the things you cannot change and have the courage to change the things you can.* Letting go of your mind's

fixed idea that you can change the loss of your husband
is a must. Coming to grips with this reality is difficult but, at some point, must be done—consciously.
What you can change is just about everything else.
This becomes the first step in avoiding fixation—the
recognition of what is in your power and what is not
and letting go of an erroneous belief. Paradoxically, in
this case, control is actually letting go.

The second step is self-awareness. I told her she
could ask herself some questions about her thoughts,
feelings, and behaviors that would help her assess her
own situation:

- Am I thinking of my pain and loss around the
  clock, in all circumstances? Am I so focused
  and preoccupied that I can't take a broad view
  of things? Has my self-preservation turned
  into self-absorption?
- Who am I, really? Of course my situation in
  life has changed, but have I traded my real
  self for a victim identity? I am *not* my pain,
  my loss, my crisis. *I am me!*
- Am I extremely intolerant of others' responses
  to me? Do I think I should be treated with
  sympathy at all times, in all situations?
- Do I have difficulty with anything new?

I reassured this mother of three small children that becoming emotionally and behaviorally entrenched in loss and grief is unusual. When I asked her if she thought she was stuck, she hesitated, as if reviewing the questions. She then promised to "think about it" but believed that she "was not." I silently agreed.

When my mother's words were stolen from her and I offered a prayer, it was not only a story about the expression of grief, but also about faith in the power of prayer. Those whose faith in God has been a part of their lives, as it has been mine, emphasized how helpful their beliefs were during their traumatic loss. Prayer—communication with God—seemed to take on an even more significant meaning at this time. A widower explained he was sure that God knew of his pain and sorrow and he felt God's care, comfort, and understanding. Another widow confirmed the experience that "comfort came quickly during my meltdowns." It wasn't that God stopped the outpouring of emotions, but after she prayed, she felt a sense that "it will be all right—this pain will not last forever."

All who acknowledged their belief in God reported the sense of His omnipresence on a daily basis, guiding them through their bereavement—a feeling of being "carried." My experience was similar, and in retrospect, this support was just what was needed at a time when grief was holding me hostage, leaving me with a broken heart and diminished brainpower. As a result of God's caretaking, these men and women described a stronger, deeper relationship with Him. A widow noted that during the days following her husband's death, her relationship with God grew stronger, and she grew closer to Him. She likened it to the first significant problem she and her husband faced in their marriage. They would talk through the issue together, drawing on each other's strength.

As the solution began to emerge, each learned he or she could count on the other in tough times. It was a reminder of the power in the maxim, *a strong bond makes the bad times half as bad (and the good times twice as good).* She said the stronger relationship caused her to trust and rely on God more through the good and bad times that followed. She is now convinced that God keeps His promise to comfort, answer prayers, and help direct lives forward.

Death tends to generate many "whys" in us. For example, we wonder about the timing. "Has God made a mistake by taking my spouse at *this* time in our lives?" On the final day of her husband's life, a wife found the answer. She said she clearly sensed that God was in control—He was in charge. As her husband was slipping away, she noticed herself taking a step back away from his bed and didn't understand why she would be compelled to do that. This enlightenment occurred long after his death as she replayed it in her memory. Perhaps there was no miscalculation, as she suspected. "I realized that this death is in God's scheme for life. He knew it was not a mistake."

Do people with religious faith heal more quickly from grief? If so, is there more than prayer and one's deeper relationship with God that makes the difference in healing from loss and mourning? Many studies have been conducted in an effort to find answers to these questions. The findings all seem to be consistent: the strength of spiritual belief is an important predictor to the length of the healing process. People who profess stronger spiritual beliefs seem to resolve their grief more rapidly and completely after the death of a loved one than do people with no or few spiritual anchors.[1]

One study found that religious people were more likely to be satisfied with their lives and to have made positive changes, such as rethinking the way they wanted to live as a result of a death. Faith seems to serve as a meaning system within which the bereaved can reframe personal loss, find coping resources, and discover areas of personal growth.[2]

Those who were left without their spouses referred to their belief in eternal life—that they would be reunited with their loved one. This conviction "sustained" them through their bereavement, adding hope to a situation that was seemingly hopeless. This idea is deeply comforting: death ends a mortal life, not a relationship, and one's spouse *does* live on. Death is not the end of existence.

Talking with an ecclesiastical leader can be comforting as well as reassuring of spiritual beliefs. Some people find it most helpful to talk with a friend or family member who has survived a similar loss. This is not a must, however. Most people have much to offer a grieving loved one, regardless of their own life experiences. Although some family members and friends may seem unsure of how to respond, they often encircle those who are trying to cope with the loss of a loved one. The impulse to reach out with love, caring, and support is strong. One widower admitted that "without my family, neighbors, and friends, I'm not sure I would have survived. I really didn't want to go on living after my wife died. Others were a life force that pulled me toward wanting to live." Perhaps an attempt to help, even though unsure of the "how," is better than no attempt at all.

Those interviewed who had older or adult children were pleasantly surprised by the reactions of their offspring. My children put their lives on hold to care for their father in his illness. It was as though the gloom of what was before us put them on auto-pilot in order to be there for him. Each made personal sacrifices, ensuring he came first. Valor at its best. I confess, I was not quite sure how my offspring, as sensitive and compassionate as they are, would react in the days following the loss of their father. None of us had ever experienced anything like this before. Their dad's death was as overpowering for them as it was for me. They were magnificent in their grief, reaching out to support me and helping to carry out the numerous details needing attention while trying to manage their own pain. Others tell of similar experiences. Whether this would be the same in all cases is unknown. The point is, children can be a cherished and unparalleled lifeline in coping with grief.

The presence of minor children can also be comforting, but they will need more comfort and care than those who are older. "I needed to stay strong for my kids. It was not their job to console me," a young widow explained. At the same time, she encouraged her daughters to talk of their grief, as she had done. Kids watch their parents handle life, and if it is too awful to talk about, it must be too awful. Death is not a secret . . . neither is grief.

Children are not miniature adults. Their way of grieving depends on their ages as well as personalities. Kids have very little experience in handling emotions of any kind, and their vocabularies limit them in expressing what they feel. It is healing for both parent and child when the young widow or widower, now being both mother and father, assists the children through their loss. Patience, understanding, and love will help them all get through the trauma.

Reviewing the coping repertoires of those attempting to survive their losses, I found several additional strategies that were commonly used. These attempts, such as physical exercise, represent a reach for life-affirming support.

There's just one big problem with exercise. I became aware of it when I met an old acquaintance whom I had not seen since Jim died. She offered the conventional greeting: How was I doing? I make it a habit of being true to myself with my response to those kinds of questions. I don't like to answer "fine" when I'm not. So I told her that it had been rough but I was doing okay—good and bad days. She suggested, out of concern, and her own experience, that I exercise. It works for her. Going to the gym or even walking can help, she said. I replied with something like, "Are you kidding? I'm just trying to put one foot in front of the other, attempting to get through the day, even the hour." She continued as though she hadn't heard (or wanted to hear) my defense: "Something happens physically." She clarified that it isn't just a way to divert attention from sorrow. Then began the explanation that I already knew, that exercise releases endorphins in our system. I started to tell her that I knew that, but she interrupted. Endorphins help people to establish a sense of well-being and cope with life's problems. I guess I didn't hear the "cope" part. I told her that I know that problems don't *disappear* through exercise.

My thoughts continued off-center from hers (I blame it on grief's brain fog). I silently acknowledged that in the past, I had noticed a boost in mood from a brisk *walk*. I have even been able to see problems differently. As she continued on, her voice seemed to fade, serving as an indistinguishable background to my wandering thoughts. I remembered what I used to tell my clients: When the body is stressed, exercise the mind; when the mind is stressed, exercise the body. There is no doubt that both mind and spirit are stressed from grief. I thanked the well-meaning woman for caring and for her advice. Silently, I stood by my point, however, that I barely had enough energy to deal with the loss of Jim at that time. Meltdowns are emotionally draining. I did consider the instruction a useful reminder. I knew she was right on. I promised myself that I would get my body moving soon—very soon. After all, I can't deny that healing *is* my goal.

Keeping busy is not necessarily exercise, but it is related—keep both the mind and the body moving. Most people said their cope chests were filled with "busy stuff" that served as distractions from the emotional pain as well as reminded them there *really is* living to do. Sometimes our mind-chatter becomes so overpowering that purposeful distractions, like a frivolous TV sitcom, can give welcome relief. As with anything in life, excess can send us orbiting out of balance. Activity, counterweighted by quiet times, is most helpful to stability. Some find the mind/body practice of yoga or tai chi to be an effective way to maintain or restore a balance of peace and mild exercise.

Music can be comforting—or not. For some individuals, especially those who have always had an appreciation and love for music, it was the warmth that nourished the soul. For me, it depended on *what* music. I found solace from only selections that were uplifting. Even though love songs had always been my preference, it was way too soon for those. It still is. I'm hopeful that will change in time.

The companionship of pets was a lifeline that many, attempting to deal with grief, found helpful. For those who are not pet fans, it is difficult to understand how a pet would be more help than hassle. For the rest of us, we understand completely. These companions seem to serve a similar (not identical) purpose to family and friends—love, comfort, and loyalty. For people who are suddenly left to live alone, a welcome from an adoring dog, tail wagging in pure joy, makes an eerily empty house a home. "He's always there to greet me when I come home, and his love is so unconditional," a recent widow explained. I agree. My little, white fuzzy dog, Abby, is my second best friend (Jim was my first), whose listening skills far exceed those of any human I have ever known.

It was interesting to discover that so many had included the coping strategy of taking care of yourself, physically and emotionally. They considered it a must—necessary to healing from traumatic loss. This seems to be a given, but not so. Although seemingly counterintuitive, it's all too easy to neglect health and wellness when so much energy is going toward an intense—and most often unfamiliar—situation. Prime examples are "forgetting" to eat and the lack of sleep that naturally occurs.

Speaking of counterintuitive, reaching out to others—giving in a variety of ways—was often mentioned as a coping mechanism for dealing with loss and grief. But how do you reach out to others when you are just trying to hold on . . . to survive? *You can't meet someone else's needs until yours are met,* so goes human behavior theory. In other words, if you are starving and finally a hamburger arrives and, at that point, you are asked to give it to another person, your ability to do so is extremely compromised. The theory provided fodder for provocative and lively classroom discussions in my human behavior classes. I was hoping the students would correctly conclude that when you are needy, it is *difficult* to meet another's needs but not *impossible.* It is extremely challenging to help others when the weight of sorrow is so heavy on yourself, but not impossible. The therapeutic value often outweighs the difficulty. Reaching out to others need not be extensive. Small efforts, such as just inquiring how someone is doing, will go a long way toward benefiting both the bereaved giver and the receiver. In the days following Jim's death, I noticed the pain on my granddaughter's face—eyes moist and searching, and lower lip tucked under the upper one. I said nothing but wrapped my arms around her. We held each other for I don't know how long in shared sorrow. We will revisit reaching out to others in a later chapter.

Most of the lifelines in cope chests were named frequently, but a few were unique and worth noting. One such example was offered by a widower of about six months. He shared his way to deal with his wife's death by experiencing her presence in his surroundings. His home was beautifully decorated with her artwork and her designer's touch. "This is how she left it. She's all around me, and I find a lot of comfort in that." His eyes told of sorrow yet comfort; his voice dropped to a whisper, "I can feel her here. She's all around me."

Coping mechanisms clearly helpful for some

were mentioned as "absolutely not helpful" to others (emphasizing the diversity of strategies). Journal writing, making scrapbooks or memory books, reading self-help books, and attending grief groups were among those in the category of *possible* helps not universally shared. Some found relief, direction, and support in individual therapy. Finally, many found profound meaning and comfort in cemetery visits while others insisted that it made things worse.

These are only a few examples of lifelines that have worked for others. It is worth repeating that each must discover what works for him or her when coping with the death of a loved one. The theme to remember that comes up again and again is *there is no one best way.* Others may help us heal, but the emphasis here is on our personal responsibility to manage our pain. Each of us is ultimately in charge of our own healing (as much as I personally don't always like to accept that).

Do men and women differ in their willingness to accept responsibility for their healing? Not really. "Responsibility" is not gender-specific. The difference, although subtle, seems to be in the way each sex copes with grief. Reports are most often generalizations—not all-inclusive. It is dangerous to assign people to categories. There are too many exceptions, and the risk of oversimplifying information is ever present. Therefore, the following discussion refers to *many*, and in some cases, *most*—not *all* men and women.

Men tend to be action-oriented in their grief. In *The River of Doubt*, Candice Millard wrote of Teddy Roosevelt's reaction to devastating loss and grief. "Each time he faced personal tragedy, he found his strength not in the sympathy of others, but in the harsh ordeal of unfamiliar challenges."[3] While Roosevelt was an *extraordinary* man, his method of coping with heartache seems to be quite *ordinary* among men. According to authorities in the field of grief and gender, men tend to grieve in an "activity" style, taking action, working through the pain by *doing*.[4] Many men are uneasy talking through their grief. When I told my male friend that I was studying grief, he matter-of-factly volunteered his advice that "all you have to do is to keep busy." (I might add he had yet to experience grief in his personal life.)

Women often seem to react quite differently and may be considered "affective" in their grieving style. They are more often feeling-oriented, and, rather than turn to physical activity, they verbalize their emotions. Women also seem to seek out social support more than men do.

The question up for debate: Does one gender more effectively deal with loss and grief than the other? To answer, the socialization of each must be taken into account. In other words, men have been socialized to act, to be physical, to do. This is the arena in which they grew up. Similarly, women were given permission to talk, feel, and operate in social groups as little girls. Both genders are comfortable in their *worlds* because it is what they know. Perhaps it is this level of comfort with their conventional behavior that makes their way of grieving effective for them.

Does this mean that males who talk through their grief, acknowledging feelings, are feminine men? And women who keep busy to outrun their grief have way too much testosterone? It is important to note that physiology and socialization *influence* gender reactions to grief but do not *determine* those reactions. Certainly, other strong influences such as personality, as well as past life experiences, are key factors. Further, neither gender is "pure" in their gender-specific reactions to life in general. We're all a bit androgynous. Mental health would dictate that both typical male and typical female lifelines for dealing with grief can be an effective part of *anyone's* cope chest (the previous discussion of the various ways people cope validates this.) Perhaps we have much to learn from each other.

Venturing outside the textbook, what more did I learn about coping with loss and grief? For one thing, I honed my knowledge about resilience. We may hear that some of the bereaved seem to be more resilient than others and wonder why. The answer is that resiliency is multifaceted. The recovery from grief is dependent upon many factors, of course. One of the most critical influences on recovery rate is a person's cope chest: first, that a metaphoric chest exists and, second, that it is supplied by each individual, personalizing its contents. Mine is stocked with several and varied lifelines that work for me. I had already known how crucial different strategies were to healing, but I didn't know the extent of possible lifelines. And those mentioned are only samples—many more are out there, being used by courageous people dealing with grief and loss.

I also learned that because there is no right length of time for recovering from grief, it is useless—and unjust—to beat up on yourself for "not getting over it" sooner. It should be no news to anyone that being kind and tolerant to yourself is definitely more conducive to healing than is self-criticism.

I now know that a *decision* to move forward must be made by those wanting deliverance from the pain of losing a spouse. How "moving forward" is defined is the challenge for each survivor. I discovered, along with others, that a forward motion is jump-started by *tuning in to living things*—such as newborn babies, rosebuds, puppies, spring rain giving way to summer sunshine followed by crisp new growth. These gifts from God and nature are literal *life*lines—reminders of life's dynamic power that still exists, offering meaning for each of us.

Triumph or *survival*? I didn't know—but I do now—that *triumph* over loss and grief is most often a bit too lofty a goal for most of us. Instead, I suggest considering going for *survival*. It is every bit as honorable and considerably more realistic.

NOTES

1. Kiri Walsh et al., "Spiritual Beliefs May Affect Outcome of Bereavement: Prospective Study," *Dept. of Psychiatry and Behavioural Science, Royal Free and University College*

Medical School, June 29, 2002, accessed July 2, 2010, http://www.bmj.com.

2. The Stress of Life: News and Articles, "People with Religious Beliefs Are More Affected by Grief, Research Shows" Ascribe—The Public Interest Newswire, April 25, 2003, accessed June 5, 2010, http://thestressoflife .com.

3. Candice Millard, *The River of Doubt* (New York: Broadway Books, 2005), 2.

4. Kenneth J. Doka and Terry E. Martin, *Grieving Beyond Gender: Understanding the Ways Men and Women Mourn*, rev. ed. (New York: Routledge, 2010).

FOUR

❦

I Didn't Know the Extent that Grief and Loss Would Change Me and My World

I have always embraced change. However, I am now and from this day forward, rethinking the "always" part. It's for sure, I've added some qualifiers. It seems like my life has been a runaway train, changing tracks at every turn, and I'm not *embracing* the journey at all. An example? Sports beget sports. Weather begets weather. It's the communication rule of the planet, known by all. When we talk of sports and weather, people respond with sports and weather. I didn't know the rule was bendable. When we talk of grief and loss, the majority of people respond with silence or by changing the subject. Confusing.

Most recently, I experienced this phenomenon when I selectively told friends and family that I was writing a book on grief and loss. These people typically participate in reciprocal conversation. I'm sure there are many reasons why with this topic, they chose to change the subject or not respond at all. The listener's discomfort is understandable, and I'm okay with it. But it's somewhat like talking to my dog (whom I genuinely respect, by the way).

I encountered the same situation four years ago. It seemed to start about two months after Jim died. Reactions of friends, acquaintances, and, yes, even family members were a bit of an enigma. Although there was obvious caring and love, many seemed lost on how to react, what to say, or how to help ease the torment. Every mourner has witnessed the shift in the dialogue—away from the recent past, to the present or future. The subject of loss is sidestepped, along with other attempts to keep the grief-stricken friend or relative from thinking about or feeling the pain of its source. The problem is, family and friends do not have the power to obliterate or divert heartbreaking thoughts or feelings. It's a tunnel that one must personally enter, and, in keeping with the common and slightly overused formula, *the only way to get over it is to go through it*. It's so applicable to grief and loss.

Talking about a deceased companion and the

emotional pain, as we know, is healing, but "who do you talk to?" the widow asks. "The subtle messages (some nonverbal) that I get are 'we love you, are concerned about you, and want you to get better, but let's not talk about it.'" This may appear to be an exaggeration, and it is in some cases, but certainly not in all.

Grief is a lonely place. In part, as a result of our culture's responses, we tend to withdraw and feel isolated. But it isn't all about people's responses to us—more often we isolate ourselves because we don't want to be around others where the demands to socialize require more emotional energy than we have. Consequently, we even feel alone in a crowd. Every person who has encountered grief eventually realizes and accepts this reality. Grief requires a large amount of courage from us. The time will come when we'll unexpectedly be aware that our courage is *rescuing* us as we reluctantly move forward.

Another of culture's messages is the expectation to resolve grief quickly and move on—the sooner the better. It seems others give the grief-stricken only a few weeks or months to get back to "normal—to their old self." It will never happen. Rather, a new "normal," a new reality, a new life is waiting, but in time. "New" is not quite accurate; it will be unmistakably *different.*

A man whose wife succumbed to a heart attack wrestled with wanting to be treated "normal" and yet have people respond to his suffering. In other words, he explained that going about his normal life helped him deal with his grief but that "people wouldn't let" him. "They kept treating me like I was fragile—they wouldn't let me be normal." Perhaps due to his own uncertainty, rooted in stress, he was sending mixed messages to those who wanted to help. We often do this when we are swept up in grief's torrent. Those in mourning are often full of conflicting thoughts and feelings. It is difficult to understand what is happening in our world and in us. Perhaps the best we can do is hope for patience and understanding from others.

The widower's conflict summarizes the confusing interaction between the bereaved and their family and friends. So many paradoxes exist: wanting to be one's old self and finding it impossible; wanting to talk through grief and loss but having no one available to listen; and needing social support but being isolated by grief.

A close friend of mine told me that after losing her husband, the reality of suddenly being single seemed like a bad dream. The nightmare kept rolling along out of her control. She clarified that the problem is going places alone where there are couples: "I felt like a misfit." She had no idea how to manage her life as a "single." She had been aware of society's need to categorize and stereotype single people but didn't know what it was like to be on the *inside*, to be one of "them." "It felt like I was wearing a badge," she added. Many others share my friend's perception, in various forms and degrees of intensity.

A related issue surfaced when a client, attempting to find a place in her familiar circle of friends, was surprised to discover that some couples had "dropped her" after her husband died. The invitations to join them came to a halt. She was somewhat confused, surprised, and saddened.

Who is likely to be more uncomfortable—the newly single person or the company of couples in her midst? If we were to examine group reactions to the newly widowed, my guess would be that the group members also experience discomfort. This is a sad commentary on our society: our existence is defined as a "couples" world. Really? How can that be when 45 percent of the country's adult population is single? Of course, a statistic is always an oversimplification, but perhaps it is time to realize that we *can* interact as individuals of worth, regardless of our relationship structure. What would happen if we changed our way of thinking? It will be months and possibly years before my friend reinvents herself as she attempts to find her way in this new, *unchosen* life. Holding on to her individuality while circumventing the "single" label may help.

The classification of single parent is a similar struggle—but not. Abruptly becoming the only parent adds a whole other layer of tests in muddling through grief. A young man who had just lost his wife to cancer was concerned: "I have a lot of worries but my biggest one is how I am going to handle my kids when they become teens. Their mother would have known." He continued, "I am so unprepared to be single as a parent as well as a single person in general. Maybe there's not a way to really prepare for something like this."

It was almost two years later that I talked with this courageous father, checking in to see how he was getting along. His children were doing well, and he had obviously moved forward and upward—not without growing pains—to meet the demands of his new role in an impressive way. Remarkable.

I received fascinating answers from my interviews when I asked, "Other than becoming suddenly single, has losing your spouse or companion changed you as a person?" All participants, without exception, agreed there had been changes, and I was somewhat surprised to discover the changes were all positive and life enhancing.

Sometimes tragedies bring out the best in people—honing individual strengths. Most survivors admit to feeling stronger as recovery progresses. The problem is they don't want to be "forced" into being strong. Society attaches a high value to strength through adversity and prefers that it be observable early on in the process. It doesn't always work that way.

Looking back at the six years since her husband died, one widow affirmed, "*I did it!*" Her fortitude carried her through the trauma and the recovery. She was a widow who wasn't sure, six years ago, that she could "do it." She was tested and passed the test. Her reward: a strong sense of self-sufficiency, an increase in self-trust and worth, and something else: courage. The grit required to weather grief's storm was now a permanent part of who she was.

I learned something similar from my journey in healing. I wasn't sure I was capable of handling something as devastating as my husband's death. But I learned that *I can do hard things.* I came to that realization in bits and pieces as I attempted to manage my pain as well as household tasks. But it was one event, orchestrated by nature, where it all came together for me.

It was a minor thing, but it turned out to have major significance. A peaceful-looking robin lay lifeless on my patio step. The unscarred body indicated it had not been attacked by another animal. Perhaps it died of old age or suffered a fatal flight into my window. At moments like these, I would call for Jim to take care of the little creature. It was always his job. I was too much of a wimp. Now it was my turn to step up—after all, this was not a big deal (I tried to tell myself). I inhaled a deep breath, hoping it would help me find inner strength. It worked. *It was a dreadfully hard thing.* I then sat down on the step, *exhaling* what seemed to be the same deep breath, head in hands and eyes closed, allowing my mind to replay what just happened. My thoughts were interrupted by the distinctive vocals of a young chickadee. As I slowly opened my eyes, there she was, a petite, splendid specimen of nature, exuberantly announcing spring. It was an epochal moment—nature's life cycle at its best and I was privileged to be a part of it. "I did it, Jim."

It seems now, at this point, I can handle almost anything. I could not have said that four years ago. Learning of one's capabilities is empowering.

Love is powerful. We know that. A widow talked of her efforts to give love and support to her husband before he died—to be there for him in any way possible. She believed her efforts helped her to "grieve less." *The love you give the living comes back to comfort you in your grieving*, she concluded.

In various ways, people responded that the death of their spouse or companion left them with an urge—and commitment—to love more . . . not only to feel more deeply but also to act on the feeling. "I'm more compassionate, a gentler person," one woman observed. "I'm more tenderhearted. I feel like I've gone through a *tenderizing process*. I find myself wanting to help others more than I did before his death. Maybe it's because so many people reached out to me when I was hurting. I have also changed in that I learned how to accept help." Similarly, another felt he had become better at valuing relationships and realizing their importance. All the widows and widowers, in different ways, echoed these changes in personal attitude. When we are so personally touched by the death of a loved one, our capacity for giving and receiving kindness seems to expand to heights never before experienced.

Those who relied on their religious faith to pull them through also talked about the part their belief played in personal changes, with comments such as, "I'm not afraid to die now. I was before," and, "I rely on God more." A widower summed it up when he said, "Going through the death of a loved one is a deep, sacred experience that changes your very soul."

Perhaps the most impactful change resulting from losing Jim, a change affecting my everyday life (and blood pressure), is that I learned the definition of a "problem." Being overscheduled or having a messy house, a broken light switch, or arthritis are not problems. They're inconveniences. I now know what a problem is. Thank goodness there are very few.

Finally, changes in family *culture* are common when death claims a loved one. A young widow, left with several children ranging from tweens to teens, felt the burden of defining the family's new reality. "We're on a new road now, but we're going to make it," she announced. She also felt the burden of being the strength of the family as she became aware that children study how their parents handle trauma and imitate it. This mother observed that the family is stronger now and that they cooperate more. "We pull together," she said, "because if we don't, we'll be torn apart."

When a spouse or companion dies, the loss demands a redefinition of our reality, whether or not we like it—and we don't. Change *is* difficult and demanding. The loss *will* change the survivors, and the change may go unnoticed at first. I discovered that the kinds of changes I *do* still "embrace" are ones resulting in personal growth. Growth can come out of positive or negative life circumstances. All change has the *potential* to enhance personal strength and development; it's our *response* to the changes that will make the difference. It is important to pause and contemplate changes in ourselves. Oftentimes, we're too quick to dwell on our weaknesses and don't dwell nearly enough on our positive growth. Perhaps that's because it feels like the loss takes so much away from us. As the widow insightfully shared, "This has been a refining process. I wish I could have made those changes without the pain." Yes, I said to myself, I too often wished for strength without struggle.

Many times during the journey through my own grief, I felt as I did watching my son play Little League football. Because of my concentrated emotional investment, I winced at every tumble, tackle, and touchdown as he bravely persevered down the hopelessly long field. Perhaps it was because I have been a participant-observer—seeing the similarities in other people's stories as I live mine. My newly discovered perspective on how grief and loss can change a person is an example. Now I clearly know how much losing Jim has altered my *life* and especially *me*. Listening to widows and widowers describe their personal changes, I've come to know the power of grief as it reaches deep into a person's character, deep enough to pull out the unexpected, such as courage.

Clearly, it takes courage to survive a devastating experience. Some say that courage is the most important of all virtues because it takes courage to act on other virtues. It is a precursor to all highly regarded personal attributes. For instance, it takes courage to love, to reach out to others, to trust yourself and those around you. It takes courage to be honest, to be patient. The courage of the men and women I interviewed was inspiring. I noticed the same spirit with friends and former clients who had lost spouses or companions. They were perfect examples of connecting with their own courage to take on "hard things," loving more, reaching out to others, and confronting the many added challenges delivered by changes in daily life.

A person can be courageous and at the same time have doubts. Courage and doubt can coexist. I learned that it takes an incredible amount of courage to stand up to traumatic change and move forward with it, even with doubts about what lies ahead. The road is not well-lit, but it will gradually become brighter with each step.

FIVE

❧

I Didn't Know If I Had a Future (and I Wasn't Sure I Wanted One)

It was as spontaneous as emotional meltdowns. No thought, consideration, or constraint. My impulsive response to Jim's death was a reflex. My place was with him. I didn't want a future without him. I was a long way from contemplating whether I even had a future. While putting all my energy into surviving hour to hour, day to day, my future wasn't even on my radar.

Defenseless, frightened, and lost, I prayed: "What now, Lord?" I had no idea, no clue. The answer came clearly and quickly: *live on.* I wasn't sure what that meant. Of course, my heart was beating; I *was* alive. I have since learned that those two apparently simple words were profoundly and deeply meaningful—but certainly not simple. For starters, I came to learn the difference between "alive" and "living."

Slowly, very slowly, I came to realize that the "on" part of "living on" meant *forward—with purpose*—and that this was the direction for me to go. It's a human thing, the instinct to evolve. It seems the *impulse to grow* is typically countered by the equal force, *resistance to change.* It is our lifelong battle. *Growing* is the victor when change forces us to confront our humanness, our propensity to progress. At that point we realize we *have* to change. From there, our discomfort pushes us toward *wanting* to change, in hopes of relieving the pain. On some level, we know that pain is the barometer of the healing process. It is then that the tide carries us to the *choosing* phase of change and personal growth, the difficult phase because it takes the most commitment and effort on our part.

Outer manifestations of our inner state often give us clues as to where we are in our progress. After a considerably long time following Jim's death, I began to make changes in my surroundings. I redecorated a major room in our home. This entailed giving Jim's classic rolltop desk away (a huge step), removing familiar art from the walls, re-covering a favorite rocker, and making other aesthetic changes in the room. Just before the last touch of new color was stitched to the lampshade, I realized that this project was a symbol of my moving forward. By the way, I also bought a new bright *red* car, not a black one.

From vacations come souvenirs—usually silly trinkets. Most of the time, these keepsakes have no intrinsic value; their worth is in their *meaning* to us, giving the past journey ongoing life. They serve as reminders of where we were at the time of purchase, bringing back warm memories. They are *symbols* of something of underlying significance, not unlike my home redecoration. When I became aware of the connection between my current behavior and my past emotional state, I realized the profound meaning in my redecoration project—and my red car. "I'm on my way," I told myself, and it feels good. (Being somewhat surprised by my discovery, I think I even said it out loud.)

I remember the time when grief was in charge—when it blazed its own trail through my days. My sense of control over my life was pretty close to zero. Now I feel in charge! Is grief still there? Grief, no (very significant). Sadness? Yes, in varying degrees, but I've learned, for the most part, to tolerate it. Emptiness? There is a hole in my heart. It is there, and always will be, because it is where memories of Jim reside. He is in my heart, and, as the song goes, "my heart will go on." I do miss him profoundly, and I know that will never go away.

At this time, I am still choosing to move forward, taking my emotions and current state of well-being with me. When do those who are grieving arrive at a similar place? Some say it is when they are able to look back at the time of death with some objectivity. Do you ever really get there? Yes, in time.

The impulse to move into our own future will be different for each of us. The significant point here is that *each person will know* when it is his or her time. You can't push the river, so the cliché goes. We'll do well to just swim with the current. When the self-propelled move forward begins, so does the realization that we were changed by that extraordinarily painful loss. We can begin, not over, not where we started, but *where we have learned.* We can use those lessons and changes as we turn away from grief and toward life. They will be attributes that will become a part of us and be with us always. I cherish the fact that I learned what a "problem" is. The challenges of daily life are met with much more acceptance and calm. It's solid. It will be that way for the rest of my life.

Moving on, for most of us, means coming to terms with memories. What do we do with them? During the days and months following the loss, memories are synonymous with pain. Barbra Streisand warns in her song "The Way We Were": "What is too painful to remember, we simply choose to forget." One widow expressed that very fear. She was deeply concerned that, in avoiding the searing memories, she might forget a great deal about her husband as the months and years went by. Perhaps the answer to these concerns is to embrace the memories slowly, through the healing process, without force or fear. When this is done, the recollections become strengthening and treasured and even invited into one's future. Memories are extremely important to our present and future well-being. The past can actually help us take the first step forward—if we grasp what it has to offer, like the realization that *today we are the sum total of our yesterdays.* There is strength and self-assurance in that maxim. We *have* had past accomplishments.

The day arrives when the increased love, attention, and caring from others fades. We realize it's time for *us* to "take the wheel." Veronica Shoffstall wrote about that day in these few lines from her poem "Comes the Dawn" (the title says it all):

So you plant your own garden and decorate
Your own soul, instead of waiting for some-
    one to bring you flowers
And you learn that you really can endure
That you really are strong
And you really do have worth
And you learn and learn . . .
With every goodbye you learn.[1]

Is it possible to *not* learn from the pain of loss?
Yes, that could happen even though it rarely does.
Anne Morrow Lindberg, noted author and wife of the
pilot Charles Lindberg, wrote:

> I do not believe that sheer suffering teaches. If
> suffering alone taught, all the world would be wise,
> since everyone suffers. To suffering must be added
> mourning, understanding, patience, love, openness,
> and the willingness to remain vulnerable.[2]

An example of learning from suffering was clear
when a client told of her husband's death. Sitting in
my office, she was puzzled at the lack of friends' invitations to socialize. "People don't call and ask me to
do things with them," she lamented. In the days and
weeks following the funeral, she had no desire to go
out and be around people—a normal and common

resistance. It was when the discomfort of loneliness triumphed over the need for seclusion that things changed. The story took a turn. She discovered that rather than waiting to be asked, she would do the asking—unpleasantly difficult, especially at first, if you're not used to extending invitations. She found there *were* "takers," people out there who were willing, even eager to "do things." She added this to her cope chest—to "*find* joy" (as she put it) and not wait for it to come to her. It was a major part of this woman's taking responsibility for her own life and well-being and vital to her continued healing. Her new mantra (borrowed from somewhere else, I believe): "If it is to be, it is up to me."

It was heartwarming and encouraging to hear the stories of grief's survivors as they worked at putting their lives back together. For starters, they had accepted that their lives would never be the same—that there would be a new normal and a new reality. They had also moved from *reactive* to *proactive* in guiding their futures. A recent widower took charge of his life by planning his days. He made sure he would always have something to look forward to. Being back in the driver's seat of his existence helped him to move beyond the dark days of grief.

When we go through life-changing experiences, others often want to identify us as "the person
who . . ." In the cases of these men and women, it was
"the person who lost her husband or his wife." Each
of us would do well to learn that it's way too simplis-
tic and artificial to become defined by one act or one
life event; needless to say, we are much more than
that. Perhaps the change starts with each of us as we
define ourselves. The loss is not who we are. We can
then project that image to others.

Moving forward requires us *to stand in the present, leaning toward the future.* Barely "leaning" is best.
It prevents us from looking too far ahead, therefore
avoiding "future panic." Runaway anxiety is a threat
when we do the "what ifs," trying to outguess the
future. This became clear to me when my circle of
friends was recently gathered in discussion about
their fear of aging and potential ill health. The topic
of nursing homes and loss of independence surfaced.
Dialogue intensified, along with emotions. The pro-
longed discussion was only exceeded by the escalat-
ing anxiety. Most of the women were years, even
decades, away from having to make those kinds of
living arrangements. Furthermore, the reality that
any of us would ever live in a skilled care facility was

remote, given the statistic that only five to seven per-cent of seniors do so, yet we'd slipped into "future panic."

The past is not off-limits. As mentioned earlier, history—all of it—is the source of who we are today, but we can't live there. It's like looking in a rearview mirror as we proceed ahead. By being in the here and now, we don't miss the joys of today—the new grandchild, conversations with new and old friends, sunsets, the touch of a hand, a warm fire. It's all a part of living.

Being present also means *letting go of grief when grief lets go of us.* Several of those I interviewed had been aware of the dangers of being attached to grief, to the pain and the suffering. They asked themselves when the sorrow left, what would take its place? Anything can become so familiar that giving it up is mysteriously threatening, an odd characteristic of humans and animals. Those I talked with knew that grief would not be smothered, pushed away, or denied; but understandably, they *did not* want to get stuck in it for years or for the rest of their lives.

I was positive that I wanted to be free from grief's shackles. In my own cope chest were several strategies that helped me to let go. I saved them for future use, when, with any luck, times would be a bit brighter—conceding that there will still be difficulties to handle. I have learned to survive with these coping methods. They worked for me, and I plan on having them available for the rest of my life. One that was exceptionally effective in getting through bereavement was to ask myself, "What would Jim want for me now?" One answer that came to mind was that he would want me to move on with my life and "be happy." ("Happy," a kind of Hallmark card word.) "Contented," perhaps, or "at peace" would be his wish for me. I would want the same for him. He would also hope for some "joy" and "gratitude." I now have all of these—most of the time. (I'm really trying, Jim.)

One other item in my cope chest came from my search for the meaning of my life without Jim. What was now the purpose of my present and future life? It seemed to have lost significance when he died. On some level, I knew I wanted to return to being a *whole person* even though it felt like a big part of me was gone. I began by identifying a direction—the mission for the rest of my life. Otherwise, days would be aimless and empty. I might also fall prey to living in the past, where my life was rich with significance.

When I finally understood the possibilities waiting ahead and how I could make the rest of my life mean something, my future seemed not only tolerable but also worthwhile. I felt energized for the first time in my healing journey. Just by acknowledging that a plan was needed, I was gently moving on.

I would design a life without Jim, in part, by drawing on my experience in helping others. I started by volunteering time in my community. I also became alert to opportunities for helping friends and family more than ever before. (This has kept me extremely busy, I might add). In addition, out of my love for music and a childhood desire to play drums, I bought a drum (friends giggled and called it "a bit bizarre") and learned how to play. All of these—the big *and* small things—gave my life the significant meaning I had longed for. I am beginning to feel like a "whole person" again.

Others may take a different route in redefining their lives as survivors. One widow who suddenly found herself a single parent to four teenage sons became active in sports, mostly cycling and hiking. She acknowledged that maybe she had subconsciously done this in an attempt to fill the role of her sons' father, who had participated in so many activities with his boys. Whether or not that was the case, she was surprised to discover how much meaning new interests added to her life. They also served to retrofit and strengthen family connections and closeness between parent and child.

Another example of redefining life after a spouse's death is that of a woman who had been so dependent upon her husband for home repairs, and for moral as well as financial support, that she was totally lost after he died. It was through the discovery of her own abilities as she took over for her husband (not happily, she wanted me to add) that she found meaning in her life. "I have done so many things that I thought I could never do. I feel unexpectedly self-confident and proud of myself." Not quite used to her newfound self-concept, she added, "I'm not sure it's okay to say that—but it's true." The next step was finding a job, not because she needed the money or even feared being alone but because she "could do most anything."

To be or not to be alone? That is the question. For many, the circumstance dictates the answer—you *are* alone. There is no question. For some, the death of a spouse or partner delivers the emptiness of living alone for the first time. For others, it may have been just a few years since they lived alone. For still others, particularly those with children at home, the household, though turned upside down with the chaotic emptiness left by the deceased, is still energized with the warmth of human relationships. Whatever the environment, adjusting to the change is a major task for all, in the present as well as the future. The differences will be in the way each makes it work for them.

Loneliness is a threat in living alone, of course. I already knew the difference between alone and lonely. By definition, being alone is an objective condition, a state of being—like being asleep—inherently neither good nor bad. It just *is*. I knew that loneliness is subjective; it's dependent on what I assign to the situation. It's like my dog, Abby, waiting by the door, relying on me to open it for her. I am the one who makes the decision on whether to honor her request. I'm in charge, and I alone will decide what is to be (much to her frustration). Knowing all of this, I finally figured out that I had intuitively chosen not to be desperately lonely in my aloneness, but I *was* desperately lonely *for Jim*. There is a difference. The clarity helped when I stumbled onto that insight. Grief and loss had made longing for Jim a natural emotional choice for me. I *did*, and still *do*, miss him every minute of every day.

Then there's the decision of whether to live out life as a "widow" or "widower." When I realized I was one of "those," it seemed as if I was the only one. Why? Currently, in the United States and other Western nations, one-third of the population sixty-five and over is widowed. It is estimated that in Western societies, half of all marriages end with the death of the husband and one-fifth with the wife's death first.

Being a widow was not my plan. I didn't sign on for this life. A "widow" is, after all, someone who needs the local Scout troop to cut her grass. I couldn't see myself as the "poor widow down the street." Throughout our fifty-one years together, Jim and I had envisioned the best scenario: we would both go together. No one would be left in pain to face emptiness and all the household chores. Neither would be soloed to orchestrate the family dynamics. Will this strange life ever feel like it fits? After four years, it still doesn't seem to fit. I'm not sure it ever will. I'm not there, yet I know I'm approaching some kind of "there." I can sense myself gradually emerging from widowhood to personhood.

Remarriage? A delicate question, though one that crosses the mind of all who are left behind. The good news is that when it does enter our thoughts, we know we are thinking self-responsibly about our future rather than denying the existence of a road ahead. Some would make a case for age as a factor in deciding to marry again. Part of their argument would be that remarriage is not for the elderly. Stories are plentiful disputing that claim. For example, three of my friends, ages eighty, eighty-two, and ninety-one each remarried after her husband's death. There are no age-related guidelines for how old a man or a woman should be to remarry (thank goodness). Certainly for those in earlier life stages there are important issues, like dating and introducing a stepparent, that require consideration if there are children in the home. Many young widows and widowers "step carefully" (rightfully so) around this one.

Some people are emphatic about never remarrying. Some may start out that way but, down the road, have a change of heart. Others may wish to remarry, especially when they feel they are ready. There is no best formula for either men or women.

Certainly, much is to be said for companionship. My friend remarried after her husband's tragic death only to be left a widow for a second time just days before my visit. The early evening light was delicate, the mood solemn yet life-affirming, as she poignantly reviewed the past years. So succinctly and with pensive grace, this widow pointed out how fortunate she had been to have married two marvelous men, both of whom she had loved deeply and equally. We *can* love again, even in our later years. We can love again without diminishing our first love. Sharing a life together—traveling, family times, hobbies, interests, and service—are meaningful, satisfying ways to live out our lives. We are never too old for new adventures. Much could be and has been written about remarriage after a spouse's death. These few pages will not accommodate extensive discussion. However, some pertinent considerations are worth noting here.

How soon should a marriage take place after a spouse is deceased? No magic number exists, but there are markers that can help with the decision. There are mileposts for accessing readiness. For example, marrying out of loneliness is a red flag. Learning to accept and manage aloneness comes first. Readiness is also dependent upon moving past grief and possible guilt. Guilt can be attached to different regrets or fears. It often comes from a desire to remarry and yet fearing that to do so would feel like infidelity. As mentioned earlier, guilt can also come with regrets of past conflicts with the deceased and things said and unsaid. These feelings must be resolved before another relationship can be successful.

Adversity introduces us to ourselves. Readiness depends on whether life's experience and gift of wisdom have given us self-knowledge and confidence. Knowing who we are gives us security as well as much-needed patience to accept others' quirks—both necessary ingredients in healthy relationships.

How to choose the right person to marry in later life is not much different than parents' advice to their eighteen-year-old, infatuated offspring. One difference is that seniors who are widowed often marry old friends, known for years. The advantage is in knowing more about the person, although there is much more to learn. How do we learn more? With time spent together, of course, but also, to use an overworked cliché, communication. Even though life has taught us the importance of talking things through, we seem to still resist and pay the price later. Among the crucial, relationship-saving topics for premarital discussions are finances, name change, friends of the former couple, relationships with former in-laws, recreational activities, future plans, daily living styles, and cemetery burial locations. Perhaps the most essential discussions would be those concerning living arrangements and children.

A widow who remarried and moved into the deceased spouse's home was surprised to find that it was like "three of us were living there." The numerous personal belongings, mementos, and pictures were just as the former wife had left them. Most disturbing, the newly widowed husband resisted moving them. "Putting them away would be like dishonoring my first wife," he insisted. His new bride was hurt, disillusioned, and frustrated. Counselors of second marriages most often advise people in this situation to select a *new* home *together* that would be *theirs*. Besides alleviating the obvious, it would be symbolic of a fresh start as a couple.

Remember what a grown-up thrill it was when you first married—the two of you—choosing your first apartment? It not only didn't matter that there were just two sparsely furnished rooms and planes that unremittingly rattled the windows as they aimed for the nearby airport. It was a magnificent home. And it was yours!

There are other possible red flags in remarriage. When I asked my friend, who was recently widowed, how his new marriage was going, he summed it up by saying, "I'm happy, but it's complicated." I asked him what he meant by that, and he said, "Kids—hers and mine." He's a man of few words, but no more are needed. So often—not always—adult children do not approve of their mother or father remarrying, or of the new stepparent, new stepsibling, or the whole package. "It's weird and unnecessary," from their point of view. Part of the translation for that response is, "What will happen to my inheritance?" "What will happen to me?" Family traditions are also threatened but need not be. They can be carried out, but with sensitivity, prudence, and careful planning. You don't need to invite all of his kids and yours to your daughter's birthday party. She will probably find more comfort and considerably more joy when "Happy Birthday" is sung by those who had done so since she was born.

The first caution when remarrying when adult children are involved is to go slow. Turn off the pressure to "blend." Parents need to lower expectations of one big happy Brady Bunch. That may happen much later, but most likely not. More commonly, and sometimes at best, children's disapproval morphs into acceptance, but it may take a while.

It's no secret that remarriage introduces weighty

changes that call for emotionally loaded adjustments. Sometimes we create change, other times things just change, and in both cases, people are transformed.

We can hope that the movement is forward. I already knew that healing and progress are possible and that progress occurs at different rates for different people. But I didn't know about the confusion that comes weeks and months after a death. In fact, the sadness often gets worse before it gets better. Nature teaches us that the darkest and coldest hour is just before dawn. It's ironic that "worse" can represent progress—but it can.

There is hope. Trust tomorrow. No winter lasts forever; no spring skips its turn. When my pain was so intense and it seemed as though it would never end, I was reminded of this metaphor. I even found a wall decoration that said simply, "SPRING," in large letters. I hung it to remind myself—I desperately needed reminding—of the newness that comes with spring and the possibility of change. Winter ends. Actually, everything has an end, except energy, which is just transformed into other configurations (so the scientists say). The lesson I learned was that spring can't be rushed, but it *does* come. I also learned that no spring is exactly the same as others we've known.

I now plant my own garden, and it's different than ever before. Author Rachel Naomi Remen wrote in *My Grandfather's Blessings*: "Every great loss demands that we choose life again."[3] There is potential energy in pain. The source of our pain is the source of our power.

So I *do* have a future. I am ready. Bring it on but don't push. I know that I have the power—and responsibility—to direct it and can do so even with lingering emotional scars. Of course, I cannot control how future events will play out, but I do have power over how I respond to those events (lesson number one from my Life Satisfaction class). I also learned, as I've gone forward, that not only is Jim a part of all that I am, but so are the memories that I have slowly allowed back into my awareness—powerful blessings that grief had kept hidden from me.

NOTES

1. Veronica Shoffstall, "Comes the Dawn," http://thinkexist.com/quotes/veronica_a._shoffstall/.

2. Anne Morrow Lindbergh, "Lindbergh Nightmare," *Time*, February 5, 1973, 35.

3. Rachel Naomi Remen, *My Grandfather's Blessings* (New York: Riverhead, 2000), 38.

SIX

❧

I Didn't Know There Was More to Helping Others with Their Grief and Loss

I didn't know what I didn't know. That's kind of how life is—a grand design. It keeps the anxiety down yet leaves us open to, and even seeking, new learning. I didn't know there was a particular skill set for helping friends and loved ones with their pain and losses. As a mental health professional working with the "public," my proficiency was in client-objectivity. When subjectivity entered the equation, it was another story. There was more to know.

Okay, so here it is: the list of "do's and don'ts." Call it "new learning," or perhaps, just "reminders." The suggestions for helping others with their grief also serve as a summary for the preceding chapters. Learning about grief firsthand, from those who have ridden the wave of devastating loss, makes for a short leap toward knowing what is needed to help others.

Such a prescriptive list doesn't seem to fit with the "do it your way" theme of this book. How can there be guidelines for helping others when we all grieve differently? Perhaps we can look to the medical field for answers. When a patient is ill with a well-known disease, such as diabetes, doctors rely on proven symptom diagnoses and treatments. However, each body reacts differently, with many factors to be accounted for. These two realities—the known facts of the disease and the differences in patients—can, and must, coexist. So it is with grief and individual responses. Being sensitive to a person's own way of grieving and accepting it are top priorities in helping the bereaved. Keeping that in mind, here are some universal guidelines that are known to be useful in helping others with loss and grief:[1]

Educate yourself on the nature of grief. Even a limited knowledge of the basics can go a long way toward guiding those who want to respond to the bereaved in a supportive way.

Be available. Share your concern. Do something rather than ignoring the person or the reality of the death. Most of us want to help others in emotional pain but feel inadequate. As a result, sadly, some do not respond at all, even though they would like to. Caregiving is simply acting on one's concern for another. It isn't always assuming a nurse's role, as we sometimes think. The "job description" simply requires giving from the heart to those who mourn. Offer support in an unobtrusive but persistent manner. Sometimes an email, call, or text is a gentle way to stay connected.

The right words may not be that important. When you're not sure what to say, sometimes just being there and saying nothing or very little is most helpful. If you are responding from the heart, with love, the nonverbal communication reaches the grieved. The messages that you are there and you care are received. Don't hesitate to use a touch, a hug, or a handclasp when appropriate. It can bring great comfort, and sometimes it is more powerful than words and is all that is needed.

Listen without giving advice. This is extremely difficult for most of us. We so want to "fix it." What most grievers really want is to talk to someone and feel that what we are saying is accepted and understood. Advice generally aborts that process. Reflective listening (listening for emotions and saying them back in your own words) can help a person feel understood.

Use caution in offering stories of your own. This can have the effect of dismissing the grieving person's pain. If you do tell of your experience, make sure the purpose is helpful to the bereaved.

Allow the grieving person to express all and any feelings, including anger or bitterness. Refrain from saying, "Don't feel that way." Frequently, sharing the way you feel is a normal (although, potentially painful) attempt to find meaning in what has happened. The author Rachel Naomi Remen explained: "Meaning is a form of strength,"[2] and "It strengthens the will to live in us."[3] People who are trying to make sense of a devastating loss certainly need all the strength possible to will themselves to live on.

Don't hesitate to mention the deceased, assuming that if you bring up the subject, it will remind the surviving spouse of the death. Be assured that the surviving wife or husband does not need reminders. Furthermore, by not mentioning the deceased, you're pretending that he or she never lived—or that's how it will come across.

Realize that no one can replace or undo the loss. Out of our deep concern, we often want to do more than "just listen." We feel so helpless. Remember that to heal, people must endure the grief process. Distressing, but true. Allow them to feel the pain—as difficult as that might be for caregivers.

Be patient, kind, and understanding without being patronizing. Don't claim to "know" what the other person is feeling. "I know exactly how you feel" is not a helpful thing to say. It's also not accurate. None of us will ever know *exactly* how another feels. This is even truer of people who have not lost a spouse to death.

Be there later, when many friends and family members have gone back to their routines. Sometimes just *being there* is all that is needed. Having contact with people who care about them over time, who do not vanish, is extremely valuable to those in mourning. Ignoring a grieving person after a short time is partly based on the flawed belief that people should "get over it" and move on quickly.

Keep promises to "call you for lunch" or "drop by to see you." You may have good intentions at the time, but all too often they are not carried out. Although this is not a major factor in the healing of grief, it certainly doesn't help. Unkept promises can come across as lack of sincerity and superficial caring. On the opposite side of the equation is the sincere invitation to go with friends and the follow-through that many widows and widowers agree is generally "welcomed" and "helpful."

Remember holidays, birthdays, and anniversaries that have important meaning for those who mourn. Again, don't be afraid of reminding the person of the loss; he or she is already thinking about it—most likely, 24-7. Approach reaching out to the bereaved gently, as the *specific* meaning of the holiday to the person is most likely unknown to you.

Avoid stereotyping. It cannot be said too many times: *be sensitive to individual differences.* Assigning thoughts, feelings, and behaviors to a grieving person is not supportive of personal growth. Many interviewees reported that being automatically assigned "lonely," "helpless," or "depressed" felt like unjust assumptions. Of course, in some cases, caretakers may be correct, but most often they are way off base. To avoid labeling altogether is to avoid offending.

Keep in mind that some people cannot, or do not want to, talk about their feelings. Don't force the issue. In many cases, when it is difficult to talk about feelings, it is much less difficult to talk of the deceased spouse or partner. It's generally therapeutic to reminisce about details of a personality, characteristics, or endearing qualities.

A story about this last point: When my husband died, my friend of many years asked, "What would you like others to know about Jim?" I cannot emphasize enough how fitting and therapeutic that question was for my emotional state. It was so sensitive and unexpectedly comforting. I felt the warmth of her words wrap around me, soothing my pain. It wasn't too long after that another friend became widowed. I never did know her husband very well, so I asked her to tell me about him. I guess my previous experience where I was the recipient of such a question was locked into my brain and heart. My friend suddenly seemed eager to retrieve a large book she had put together for her husband before he died. It was his life story in words and pictures. She had never shown it to anyone before and was eager to take me through, page by page. I sensed her response to my asking. It was the same as mine had been when roles were reversed. Perhaps this was one of those "pay it forward" opportunities even though it was without my conscious intent. A footnote to the story is that this is a friend who had a lifetime of difficulty expressing feelings verbally. This time her emotional message was unmistakably clear as she turned each leaf of the memoir, which had obviously been created with intense devotion.

Expressing feelings of sympathy to a friend or loved one who is grieving can also be difficult. We do want to respond in a helpful way but worry about saying or doing something "wrong." When in doubt, ask. One of my family members had those doubts, so after her initial response to my loss, she asked me what I found helpful. She added, "Does talking about Jim help or hurt?" The message was one of deep caring and sincerity. This approach may be more useful with close relationships—those with a history. "How can I help?" is not the same thing. There is a subtle difference. The focus in the second example is on the caregiver; the first, on the bereaved.

We are not cows. Yet we can know a lot about milk—enough to nurture ourselves and others. Pause and consider the cow with her soft eyes and docile manner, accepting all around as they are. Consider what we can learn from her. Have you ever known any living creature more patient and tolerant than a cow? Healing would best be served if the bereaved and those offering comfort were patient, tolerant, and understanding with themselves and with each other. As caregivers, we occasionally, unintentionally say and do the "wrong" thing. Those struggling with grief and loss are vulnerable to a variety of emotions and behaviors, even irritation and criticism. Condemnation of a caregiver's efforts can slip out unnecessarily. Perhaps a deep breath mixed with tolerance is needed on both parts. We all need "slack." After all, are we not, with our imperfections, living a life of "learn as you go"?

And as I have gone, I have learned a startling amount about loss and grief. Like the widow who would have designed it differently, I too wish I could have learned it without the pain. I did become aware that as grief grew weaker I grew stronger, in some ways even surpassing where I was before the journey began. I learned the difference between "knowing of" and "knowing" grief. I now know that grief is extremely powerful, has a life of its own, and is messy, complex, intensely painful, and life-changing. I know that I needed to trust my own way of grieving. My desire is to use my new understanding to help others in the future.

I have become more acutely (and painfully) aware

that, if we live long enough, we'll experience grief and sorrow. Loss, whatever its nature or degree, is impossible to escape in life. And loss will most likely bring grief. It is a normal and unavoidable reaction. Yet we don't have to live long at all to find out how to help others through their bereavement. We can know more, if we choose to.

Perhaps the most consoling fact, confirmed by personal experience, is that grief is time-limited. The time is different for each of us, and that is how it should be. Even the scars grief leaves are tolerable. I learned it is possible to survive—not only survive, but also to grow through loss. The impulse to grow is as strong as the impulse to survive.

I know.

NOTES

1. Family Caregiver Alliance National Center on Caregiving, "Fact Sheet: Grief and Loss," accessed June 5, 2010, http://www.caregiver.org.
2. Remen, *My Grandfather's Blessings*, 170.
3. Ibid., 29.

ACKNOWLEDGMENTS

For encouragement, generosity, and guidance I am eternally grateful—

Beginning with Jim, whose love lived on to keep me warm during grief's bitter chill . . . and beyond.

To all of those who were widowed, for their strength and willingness to share their stories so that others may not feel alone.

To Jeri Parker, who, like a superbly skilled and patient horse whisperer, gently tamed my writing. (Did I say that correctly, Jeri?)

To a special friend, who through her own pain and with her magnificent mind logged in brainstorming hours, guiding the ideas for this book over the kitchen table.

To my children and grandchildren, who

surrounded me like a tourniquet, compressing my pain.

To the publishing team at Cedar Fort for their expertise, confidence, and efforts to organize me.

To my former students who, in spite of suffering through lectures on "cows" and other anthropomorphized lesson objects, went on to become outstanding professionals.

To former clients who taught me about the courage to change.